The FIRST BOOK of
TRAINS

GRATEFUL THANKS from the author to many railroaders on the job who obligingly "talked shop," to Mr. H. W. Haynes and R. E. Woodward for providing access to a diesel road locomotive, and to Thomas J. Sinclair and staff of the Association of American Railroads for pointing out original sins of commission, omission, and expression in the text.

SBN 531-00655-7

17   18

Printed in the United States of America

Library of Congress Number: 55-7782

THE **FIRST BOOK** OF
TRAINS

by **RUSSEL HAMILTON**
Pictures by **JEANNE BENDICK**

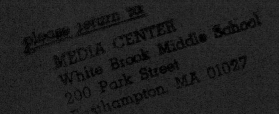

FRANKLIN WATTS, INC.
575 LEXINGTON AVENUE
NEW YORK 22, N. Y.

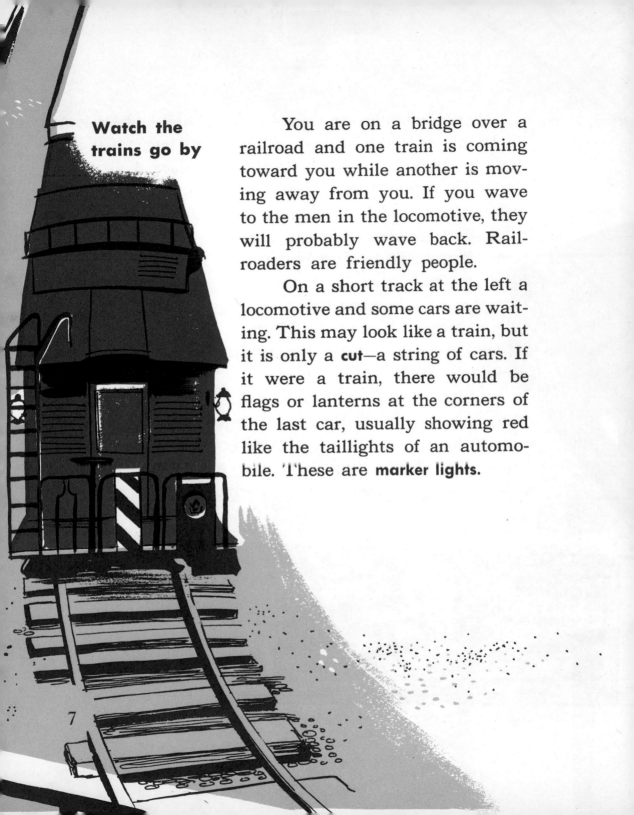

Watch the trains go by

You are on a bridge over a railroad and one train is coming toward you while another is moving away from you. If you wave to the men in the locomotive, they will probably wave back. Railroaders are friendly people.

On a short track at the left a locomotive and some cars are waiting. This may look like a train, but it is only a **cut**—a string of cars. If it were a train, there would be flags or lanterns at the corners of the last car, usually showing red like the taillights of an automobile. These are **marker lights.**

7

You can tell many things about trains just by looking at them. If the engine carries green flags, it means that the train is in two sections. The **second section** is following. At night this engine would have a green light in addition to the flags. If the flags and lights are white, the train is an **extra**—one that is not on the railroad timetable. If the engine does not show any flags or marker lights, the train is one of the railroad's regular daily trains.

Some trains have fine-sounding names, like "Twentieth Century Limited," or "City of San Francisco," but all trains have numbers. Engines have numbers, too, and most of the cars you see.

Most of the trains you will see are either **freight trains,** which carry things, or **passenger trains,** which carry people, baggage and mail, like as not. Sometimes a railroad **work train** comes along carrying railroad workers and their equipment to places where they are needed.

SOUTHERN
23488

CAPY 10000
LD LMT 1200
LT WT 41100

Freight trains are made up of freight cars that rock and rumble as the train clatters by. There may be as many as a hundred or more cars in a freight train. It is not unusual to see one that is a mile long!

Most freight cars are painted black or red or yellow. They may be from twenty-five to seventy-five feet long and about ten feet wide. On their sides are letters and numbers to tell when they were built, how much they weigh, and how heavy a load they can carry. There are also designs or advertising slogans painted on the sides. These are the **heralds,** or emblems, of the railroads which own them.

Passenger trains have cars with rounded roofs and smooth sides. Some of them are painted in different colors and some are decorated with colored stripes. There are even whole trains of gleaming stainless steel cars.

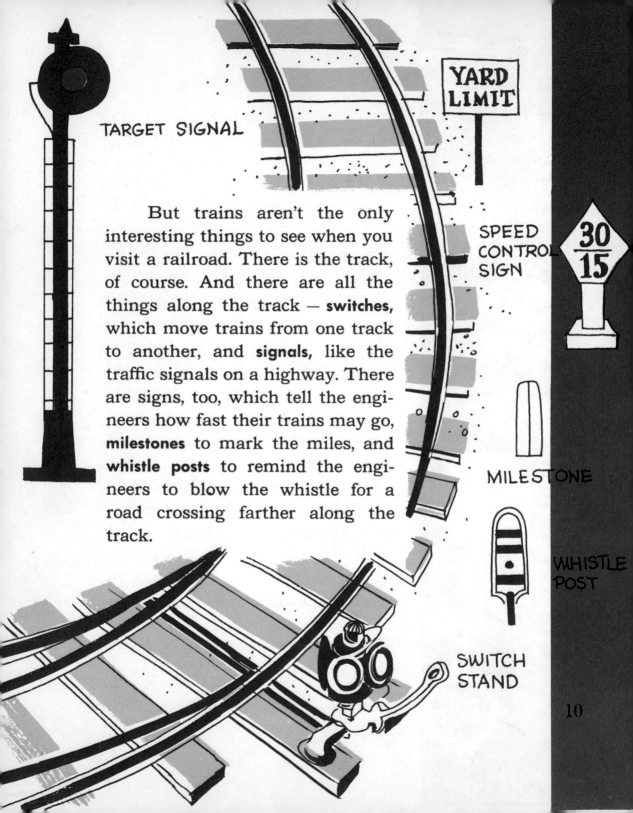

TARGET SIGNAL

YARD LIMIT

SPEED CONTROL SIGN

30
15

MILESTONE

WHISTLE POST

SWITCH STAND

But trains aren't the only interesting things to see when you visit a railroad. There is the track, of course. And there are all the things along the track — **switches,** which move trains from one track to another, and **signals,** like the traffic signals on a highway. There are signs, too, which tell the engineers how fast their trains may go, **milestones** to mark the miles, and **whistle posts** to remind the engineers to blow the whistle for a road crossing farther along the track.

Trains that carry things

There are several kinds of freight trains. **Way freights** pick up cars waiting to join trains. **Time freights** stop at only the big cities and towns. **Dispatch freights** are special freight trains that run long distances and often over more than one railroad.

Almost all cars have two four-wheel swiveling **trucks** to support the **car frame.** The car frame is usually a big steel beam running the whole length of the car. Laid across it are cross beams, to which the floor of the car is fastened.

Between the wheels of a freight car you can see the **brake shoes.** The **brake gear** — pipes, hoses, levers and chains fastened to the frames and the trucks — makes the brake shoes press against the wheels to slow or stop the train.

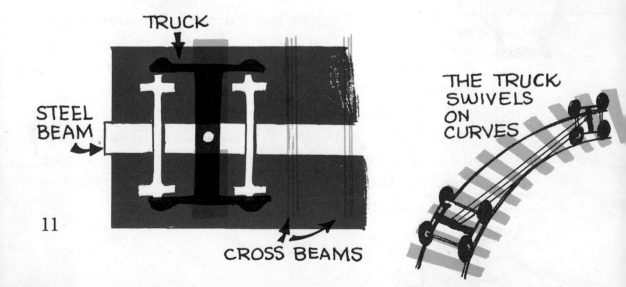

TRUCK

STEEL BEAM

CROSS BEAMS

THE TRUCK SWIVELS ON CURVES

11

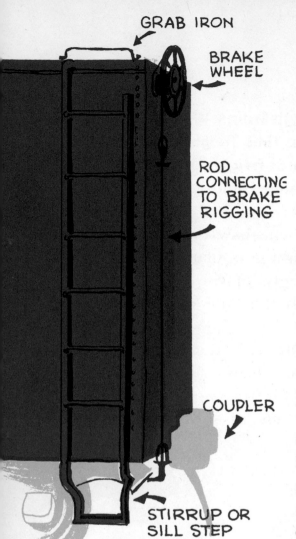

GRAB IRON

BRAKE WHEEL

ROD CONNECTING TO BRAKE RIGGING

COUPLER

STIRRUP OR SILL STEP

At one end of every car is a small iron **brake wheel** joined by rods and chains to the brake rigging underneath. This works the brakes when the car is not in the train.

At the corners of most freight cars there are ladders and stirrups. The trainmen use these to climb aboard the cars or onto the **roof walks,** where they sometimes go when they want to signal messages to the engineer in the locomotive.

Fastened to the sides and ends and tops of the cars are metal handholds called **grab irons.** The grab irons are in the same places on all cars so that the trainmen can find them even in the dark.

At each end of every car a big lump of metal sticks out. It is shaped something like a hand held half open and it is known as a **coupler.** The couplers grip each other to hold the cars together. When a trainman moves a lever on the side of the car, the coupler will open so that the car can be pulled away.

12

COUPLERS' GRIP

At the end of most freight trains there is a funny little car called the **caboose.** This is the office and sometimes the overnight home of the trainmen.

Outside, the caboose looks like an oblong box with platforms and doors at each end. It has windows, and a chimney sticking out of the roof. On top of the caboose is a cupola—a small, square structure with windows through which the trainmen can look out over the train. Some very new cabooses have bay windows in the sides.

Inside the caboose are seats, a table, a water cooler, a washstand, a stove, and lockers where the trainmen can store their own things and keep train supplies like flags and lanterns. There are even bunks for them to sleep in.

NOW, MANY CABOOSE CARS HAVE A "BAY WINDOW."

Cars for different things

BOX CARS ARE THE
WORKHORSES OF THE
RAIL ROAD.

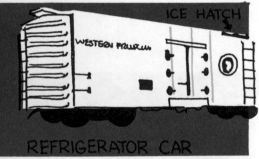

REFRIGERATOR CAR

STOCK CAR

The reason all freight cars do not look alike is that they are made to carry different things. There are more BOX CARS than any other kind. They carry almost any freight that must be protected from the weather. Fresh fruits and vegetables travel in special refrigerator box cars called **reefers**, or **freezers**. Live animals, like cows and chickens, travel in other special box cars with lattice-like sides. These are called **stock cars.**

FLAT CARS carry things that are too big for box cars and that bad weather won't hurt. Logs, army trucks and farm machinery are some of the things that travel on flat cars.

FLAT CAR

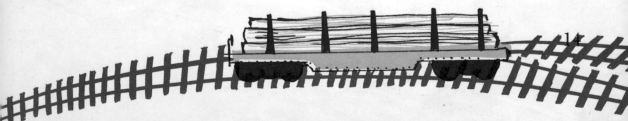

14

HOPPER CARS have slanted bottoms that open. They carry coal, sand, ore, crushed stone, or anything else that can be unloaded by dumping. Long hopper-car trains of coal are called **black snakes**.

GONDOLAS look like flat cars with sides added. They carry the same loads as hopper and flat cars.

TANK CARS carry liquids such as oil, chemicals, vinegar, and milk. There are even pickle tank cars! Some tank cars have domes on top where the liquids are pumped in.

Full trains of flat cars carrying truck trailers are called **piggy-back** trains.

PIGGY-BACK CAR

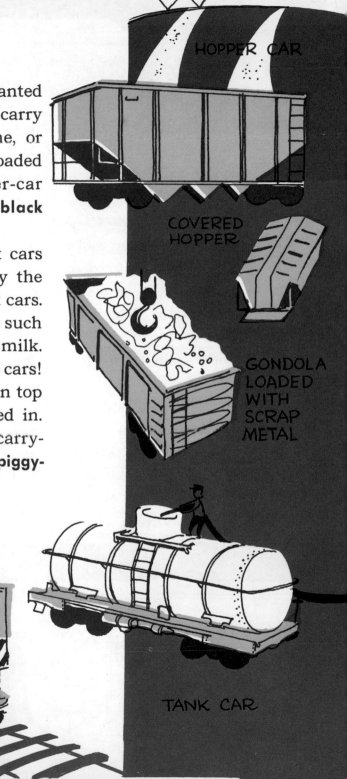

HOPPER CAR

COVERED HOPPER

GONDOLA LOADED WITH SCRAP METAL

TANK CAR

Trains that carry people

Thousands of Americans travel back and forth to work each day in **commuter trains,** which are made up of nothing but **coaches.** Coach cars have steps at either end leading to a covered platform, or **vestibule.** Between the cars a covered framework called a **diaphragm** makes a short, safe passageway for people to walk through.

Inside each car there are two rows of seats separated by a center aisle. Each seat holds two people. Some modern coaches have seats that you can adjust to the position you like best. Most modern coaches are air conditioned, too. When you travel by coach, the **conductor** punches your ticket and tells you when you come to the station where you want to get off.

16

THE RAIL DIESEL CAR IS A
COMPLETE TRAIN IN ITSELF,
BUT CAN BE JOINED WITH
OTHER RDC'S TO MAKE
MULTIPLE UNIT TRAINS.

Commuter trains are also called **locals,** because they stop at every station. But a local is really any train, freight or passenger, that makes many stops. Some of the new local trains are just one car. These new RDC's—Rail Diesel Cars—are eighty-five feet long. They have built-in motors to make them run.

Passenger trains that skip all but the larger cities and towns are called **express trains.** In an express train there are usually several kinds of cars. One of them is the **baggage car,** with big sliding doors in its sides. Here the **baggageman** rides to look after the passengers' trunks and suitcases. If you take a trip with your dog, it will ride with the baggageman.

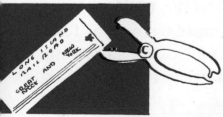

17   EVERY CONDUCTOR'S
     PUNCH MAKES A
     DIFFERENT-LOOKING
     HOLE

Millions of letters and parcels travel in special cars in express trains. These cars are marked "U. S. Railway Post Office." They look just like post offices inside, and the men who ride in them sort the mail and cancel stamps just the way the mailmen do in the post office in town.

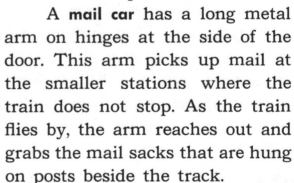

A **mail car** has a long metal arm on hinges at the side of the door. This arm picks up mail at the smaller stations where the train does not stop. As the train flies by, the arm reaches out and grabs the mail sacks that are hung on posts beside the track.

Railway Express cars travel in express trains too. They are like baggage cars except that they carry shipments for the Railway Express Agency, a company owned by the railroads.

18

If you take a trip lasting more than a day, you will probably ride in a passenger car called a **Pullman**, named after George Pullman who built his first sleeping car in 1859 to make traveling easier for people who had to make trips lasting overnight. Pullman **sleepers** have seats that can be turned into beds and Pullman **parlor cars** have homelike, comfortable chairs and tables.

Modern all-Pullman trains are traveling hotels, with bedrooms and compartments for families, roomette berths for one. You eat in a restaurant, the **dining car**, and may relax in the parlor **lounge car** afterward. Perhaps there will be movies and games in a special car, and a secretary and a barber on board. A Pullman **porter** is always on duty in each sleeper.

THE CHAIRS IN A PARLOR CAR ARE LIKE LIVING-ROOM CHAIRS.

19

A DINING CAR HAS A KITCHEN,

AND A DINING ROOM.

YOU CAN HAVE A BEDROOM ON A PULLMAN.

"STANDARD" COACH

DINER

COACH

These typical modern passenger cars carry people, luggage, express, and mail.

DOME CAR

From the glassed-in **cupola** on top of this car you can watch the scenery and the cars ahead.

PULLMAN

AMELIA

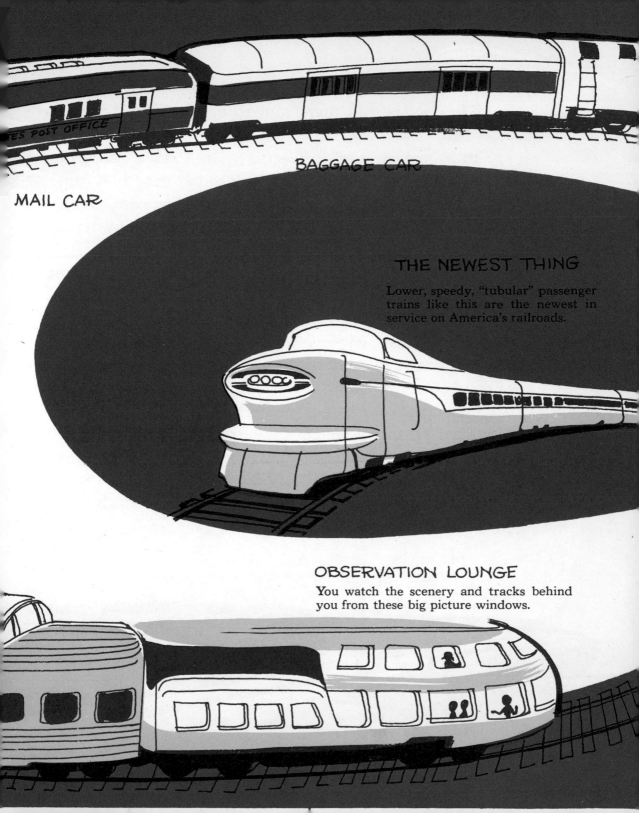

MAIL CAR

BAGGAGE CAR

THE NEWEST THING

Lower, speedy, "tubular" passenger trains like this are the newest in service on America's railroads.

OBSERVATION LOUNGE

You watch the scenery and tracks behind you from these big picture windows.

Which came first, the trains or the track?

The fact is that there had to be track before trains could run.

In a book printed in Germany in 1519 a crude picture shows a narrow track and freight car used in a mine. A number of such "rail ways"—as they were first called —were made in Europe, England, and America by laying planks end-to-end in two lines just far enough apart to match the distance between wagon wheels. To keep the planks in place the builders fastened them to heavier planks called **crossties,** or **ties,** laid crosswise underneath. These short rail ways were very useful in mines and quarries, but it was not until the 1800's that there was anything like the railroads we have today.

During the early, early years of rail ways someone thought of putting a **flange**—an extra lip of metal—around the inside edge of each wheel. Then it was easier to keep the wagons on the track. Someone else thought of fastening each pair of wheels solidly to the axle so that the axle and the wheels moved together and the wheels did

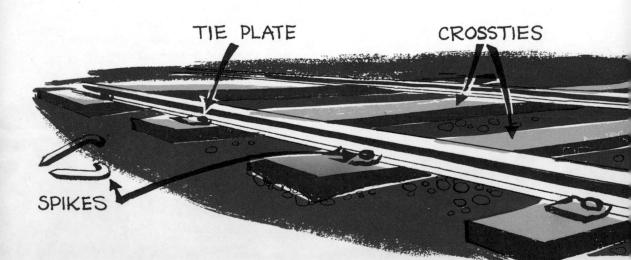

TIE PLATE   CROSSTIES

SPIKES

not wobble. Then switches and **turntables** were invented. Switches have movable pieces of track that let trains go from one track to another. Turntables are sections of track that revolve over a round pit to turn cars and engines around at the end of a railroad.

Railroad builders tried many different materials before they discovered that metal makes the best **rails.** But nobody has found a better material than wood for the ties.

The track which trains run on today is made of long, T-shaped steel rails that rest on wooden ties, just as the planks did long ago. The rails are fastened to the ties with big nails known as **spikes.** The spikes are hammered into the ties through metal plates called **tie plates.** These keep the rails from cutting into the wooden ties. The car wheels roll on top of the rails, and the metal flanges around the inside of each wheel guide them on the rails so that the engineer can drive without steering.

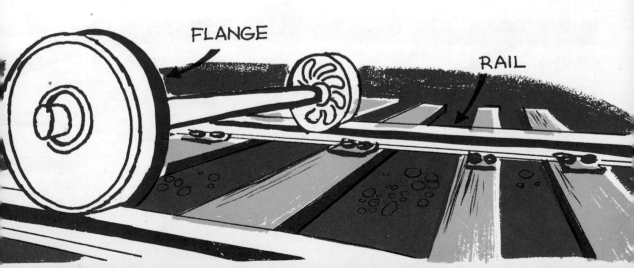

FLANGE

RAIL

Why railroads go where they do

When you visit a railroad, you see only a small part of it. If you went up high enough in an airplane you· could look down and see thousands and thousands of miles of track stretching like a big spider web over the country. You can see the same thing if you look at a railroad map. There will be many long, strong lines that cross at important cities. These are the **main lines** of railroads, and they usually stretch for hundreds of miles between two important places, such as two big cities. The ends of the main lines are called **terminals**. Between the terminal stations are smaller **way stations** where the trains may stop.

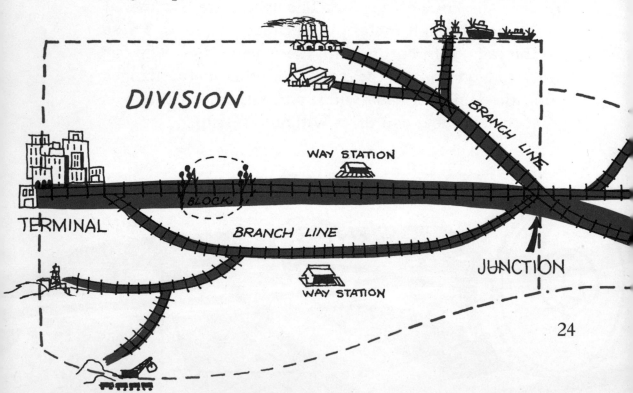

You will also see shorter lines branching off the main lines to smaller places. These **branch lines** act as feeders to the main lines. They bring to them the products of mines or farms or factories. If you look at a railroad map a few years from now, you may find that some of the old branch lines are gone. New ones may be added. This is because railroads go only where they are needed.

Sometimes a main line splits or branches at an important station so that some trains can go to stations that are not on the main line. The stations where these branching lines begin are called **junctions.** Junctions are also places where railroads come together or cross each other.

Because railroads are so long, railroaders find it easier to **operate,** or run them, if they divide them into parts which they call divisions. Each division has a big station called the **division point.** Here the railroaders who operate that part of the railroad have their offices. The divisions are divided into still smaller parts called **blocks.**

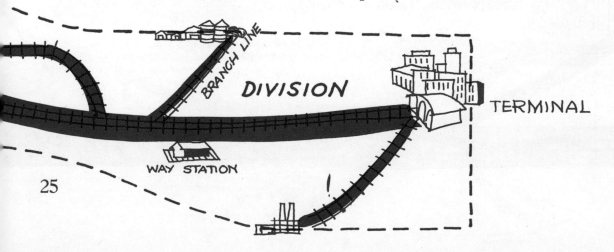

BRANCH LINE

DIVISION

TERMINAL

WAY STATION

Sometimes a special track curves away from the main line to a place like a coal yard, a lumber yard, or a factory. This is a **spur,** where cars are pushed to take on or deliver their loads.

Shorter lengths of track that run for a little way beside the main track are **sidings.** When a fast train has to pass a slow train going in the same direction, the slow train runs onto the siding and waits for the fast train to pass.

Both spurs and sidings are connected to the main track by switches. When a trainman wants to move a train onto either one of them he **throws a switch,** like this:

Near the station there may be whole groups of tracks branching off the main track. These tracks are like dead-end streets. They don't go anywhere! At the end of each one there is a strong, solid **bumper** to keep the cars and locomotives from running off the track. Many sidings make the **railroad yard,** where cars wait until they are ready to be used in trains.

SPUR

Crossover, joining the two main tracks, makes it possible for trains on either one to pick up or set out cars in the spur and yard.

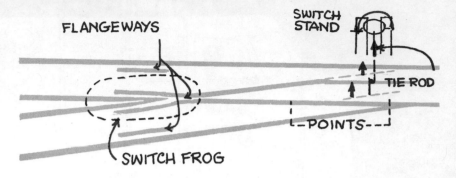

FLANGEWAYS

SWITCH STAND

When trainman turns handle of switch stand it moves the tie rod, which in turn moves the switch points. Dotted lines in diagram show where points move to let a train take the turnout.

TIE ROD

POINTS

SWITCH FROG

Because most railroads have dozens of trains running in opposite directions, a main line may well have two tracks. Then **opposing trains**—those going in opposite directions—can pass each other without stopping. One track may be called the east-bound main and the other the west-bound main. Or they may be called the north- and south-bound mains.

At very busy parts of the railroad the main line may have four tracks — two going in one direction, two in the other. Then there will be **crossovers** — two connecting switches — to let trains cross from one track to another. Now two trains moving in the same direction can pass each other, and a third train can also pass by switching from track to track around the first two trains.

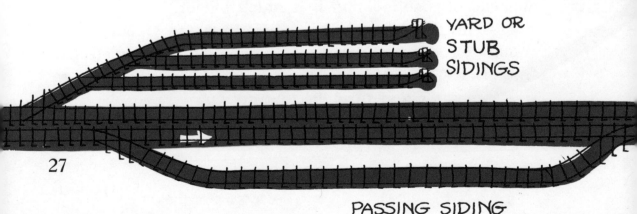

YARD OR STUB SIDINGS

27

PASSING SIDING

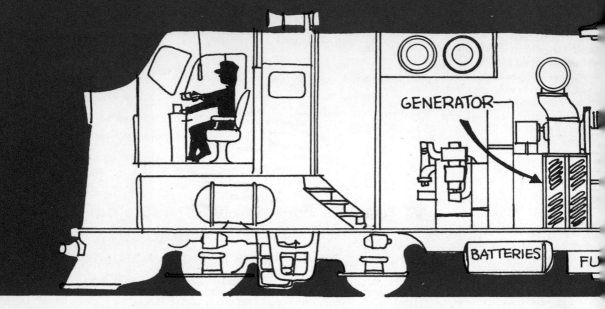

GENERATOR

BATTERIES

FU

Locomotives are power

Railroaders call the great engines that pull trains "power." For one hundred years the power to move trains was supplied chiefly by **steam locomotives**. Today you will see more and more of the great **diesel-electric locomotives** we call **diesels**.

A diesel is really two engines in one—a diesel engine and an electric engine. The diesel is something like the motor in an automobile except that it burns fuel oil instead of gasoline, and it is much bigger.

The diesel motor drives a **generator**—a machine that makes electricity. From the generator wires go to electric motors called **traction motors,** which take electricity from the generator and turn the locomotive's wheels.

Inside the locomotive other machines help the diesel

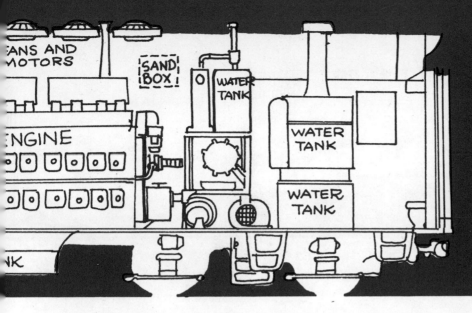

motor, generator and traction motors run smoothly without getting too hot when the locomotive goes fast or pulls a heavy load or brakes to a stop.

There are also electric batteries for starting and lighting. Tanks and boxes hold fuel oil, lubricating oil, water and sand. Big pipes and little pipes and two miles of wire join all these things so that they work together. Some diesels even have a steam generator or boiler for heating.

With all there is inside it, no wonder a diesel locomotive rumbles, snorts, pants, growls, whirrs and hums!

"Little" diesels weigh as little as 44,000 pounds, or twenty-two tons. A big one may weigh 594,000 pounds! The big diesels can move at a crawl or tear along at 90 to 110 miles an hour.

29

DIESELS
AND WHAT THEY DO

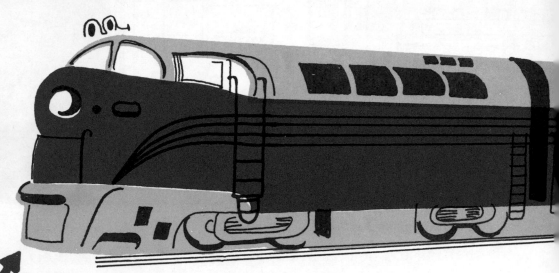

Road Engines pull heavy freights and swift passenger trains on the main line. They are from 50 to 70 feet long, about 10 feet wide and 15 feet high. They weigh as much as 316,500 pounds. Some pull only passenger trains and can go 117 miles an hour. Others handle only freight trains and have power rather than speed. Still others are built to handle both passenger and freight trains and are called dual-purpose locomotives.

Switchers bustle back and forth in railroad yards and on branch lines whenever there's a job of making and breaking up trains or spotting cars on sidings. The first diesels used in America, in 1925, were switchers.

Road Switchers are the short-haul work horses. They are used in local passenger and way freight service where switching is part of the job. Coupled together, road switchers can be used as a single road engine.

Smallest diesels are these **dinkies**, even though the littlest one may weigh 20 tons! These little diesels are popular with railroads that must move short cuts of cars in and out of factory sidings where there are very sharp curves.

Big diesels get bigger by adding units, each a complete package of power. The "A" units have cabs for engineer and fireman. These units may be coupled back-to-back as a two-unit locomotive. "B" units—without cabs—may be sandwiched between "A" units to make a three- or four-unit locomotive that can pull a mile-long train, fully loaded.

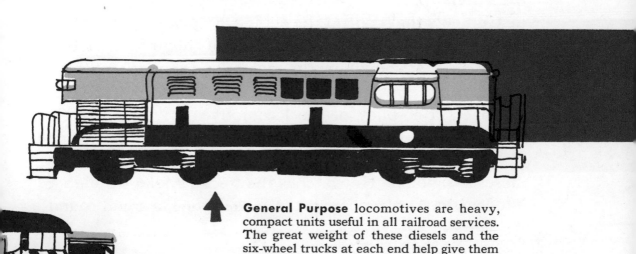

General Purpose locomotives are heavy, compact units useful in all railroad services. The great weight of these diesels and the six-wheel trucks at each end help give them extra power for their size. They are only about as big as a road switcher.

Fireman Scotty sits in the left side of the locomotive cab. Before the train starts he'll check the engines in each locomotive unit and prepare the engine and train classification lights. Once the train is moving he stays in the cab.

Lords of the locomotive

The **engineer** and the **fireman** are the lords of the locomotives. The engineer drives and the fireman is his helper. The fireman got his name from the days when he had to take care of the fire in a steam locomotive. Both the engineer and the fireman ride in the **engine cab**— the special part of the locomotive where the levers and instruments that control the engine are placed. On diesels, it is the fireman's job to watch over the gauges and meters in the cab that show how the motors and other machinery are running. Out on the main line he is really a co-engineer, or co-pilot, of the locomotive.

Engineer Casey climbs the outside ladder and takes the padded seat at the right-hand side of the cab of his diesel locomotive. He watches the tracks ahead through a windshield. At his elbow is the **control stand,** a small round

Engineer Casey is at the locomotive controls in the righthand side of the locomotive cab. After the conductor, he is the boss of the whole train. Most engineers are firemen before they are engineers.

tower with levers sticking out of it. The top lever is called the **throttle.** Casey moves it back and forth with his left hand to make the engine go fast or slow. Below the throttle is the **reverse lever,** which makes the engine go forward or back up.

Casey keeps his right hand on the **brake levers,** which he moves to work the brakes of the engine and the train. When he wants to know how fast the locomotive is going, he looks at a **speed recorder** below the windshield. He pulls a cord dangling from the ceiling to blow the **air horn.**

Before his train starts Casey tests the controls and brakes to be sure they are working right. Then he moves a lever that blows sand onto the tracks to keep the wheels from slipping. Fireman Scotty checks the motors and Casey listens to see if they sound right.

THE ENGINEER AND THE
CONDUCTOR COMPARE
WATCHES BEFORE
THE TRAIN STARTS.

Engineer Casey needs to know the **consist** of his train—how many cars there are, what kinds, and how many are loaded or empty. Conductor Jackson, the captain of the train, tells him this. When a train pulls out, Jackson may wait near the track until the last car comes up to him. Then he can swing himself aboard with the grab iron.

Brakeman Joe and Brakeman Bill help the conductor watch over the train. These men are called brakemen because on the old trains their job was to work the brakes by hand. Brakeman Joe may ride in the locomotive to watch over the train from the head end. He is the head-end brakeman. Brakeman Bill, the rear-end or

34

"parlor brakeman," climbs into the cupola on the caboose to watch over the rolling train ahead. If anything goes wrong, the trainmen will warn Casey and he will stop the train.

More and more trains today have telephones that connect the locomotive cab and the caboose. This is so that the men in the front of the train and the men in the rear of the train can talk to each other quickly when they need to. But Casey and Jackson, and Bill, Joe, and Scotty too, can talk back and forth in the same way trainmen have talked for years—by **hand signals**. Then at night they can make signals with lanterns or flashlights.

CAN TALK,
BY PHONE

WITH BRAKEMAN BILL
IN THE CABOOSE.

35

If Casey has to take the train onto a siding, Joe is the one who will get off, run ahead, and throw the switch. But both brakemen have to protect the train if it has to make an unexpected stop out on the main line. Bill will go down the tracks behind the train. Joe will go out ahead of the train. Then they will **flag down** or stop any train that comes toward them on the same track. In the daytime they will use red flags. At night they will use burning red flares or **fusées**. When their train is ready to go again, Casey will **whistle back** the brakemen by a signal of four or five blasts on the diesel air horn.

BRAKEMAN'S
SIGNALLING
EQUIPMENT

HAND
FLAG

LANTERN

FUSEE
BURNS
BRIGHT
RED

TORPEDO ON
RAIL BANGS
OUT A WARNING
TO THE FOLLOWING
TRAIN

Conductor Jackson works at the table in the caboose. He has a ticket or **waybill** for every car in his train. The waybill tells where the car came from, what's in it, and where it is going. Jackson must deliver the right waybill with every car or shipment at the end of the run.

Engineer Casey and Conductor Jackson have a special timetable called an **operating timetable** which tells them what other trains are moving along the railroad with their train. This big operating timetable gives the regular schedules of all the passenger and freight trains. All the trains are numbered and labeled, or **ranked.** Trains that are ranked as **superior,** like any of the fast streamliners, have the right to pass any trains they meet or catch up with along the line. The direction in which a train is traveling counts toward whether it is superior or inferior, too. But the superior direction may not be the same on every railroad.

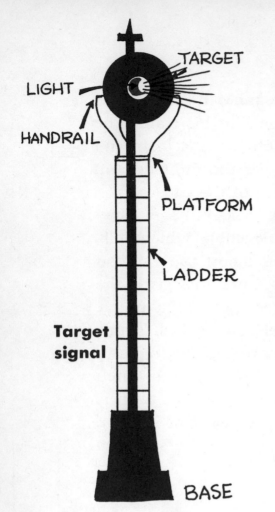

TARGET

LIGHT

HANDRAIL

PLATFORM

LADDER

Target signal

BASE

Railroad signals

Casey and Scotty must watch the signals along the track very carefully, just as an automobile driver must watch the traffic lights that tell him when to stop and go. Railroad signals are lights or movable metal arms. They are attached to poles at the right-hand side of the track, or to **signal bridges** across the tracks.

The arm signals are called **semaphores**. Semaphores have lights, too, so that they will show at night.

Semaphore signals

Some kinds of signals and what they say

go

slow down

stop

Position lights

TARGET AND COLOR LIGHT SIGNALS

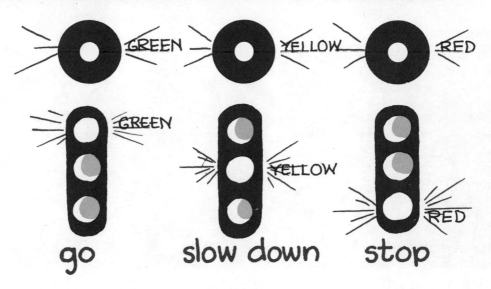

go slow down stop

Interlocking signals are often put on signal bridges over the tracks and with an interlocking tower near by.

HAND AND LANTERN SIGNALS

REDUCE SPEED

STOP   GO   BACK UP   APPLY THE BRAKES   RELEASE AIR BRAKES

WHISTLE TALK

● means a short toot

▬ means a long toot

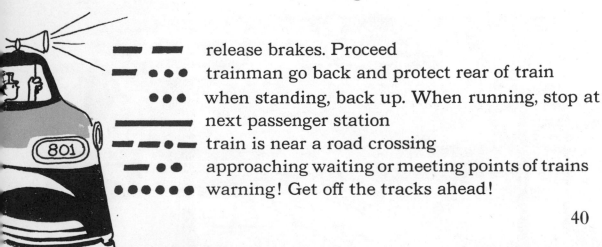

▬ ▬ ▬   release brakes. Proceed

▬ ● ● ●   trainman go back and protect rear of train

● ● ●   when standing, back up. When running, stop at next passenger station

▬   train is near a road crossing

▬ ▬ ● ▬   approaching waiting or meeting points of trains

● ● ● ● ● ● ●   warning! Get off the tracks ahead!

40

There are signals at the beginning of each block of a railroad division or section. When Casey's train enters a block, the signal flashes red to tell any train that follows that the block has Casey's train in it.

Casey and Scotty read the story of the signals aloud. "Clear board," says Casey when he sees a green signal ahead. "Clear board," Scotty repeats when he sees the green signal. But if the signal had turned red right after Casey saw it, Scotty would have said "Red board," and as soon as Casey saw the red signal he would have said "Red board," too. Then he would have stopped the train. Some railroads use yellow-colored signals, meaning "Caution"—slow down—along with the red and green signals.

41

These railroad signals work by electricity. When a train or an engine is in the block, electricity flows through the track, with wires connecting the rails to the signals. The electricity moves the parts of the signal that flash a warning to trains coming into the block.

Often at places where there are many tracks, switches, crossovers, and sidings, the signals are wired to **signal towers** beside the track. Now they are called **interlocking signals**. Railroaders called **towermen** watch from the towers and keep a record of every train that passes. They can work the signals by moving levers right in the tower. When a train must switch onto a siding or from one track to another, the towermen move other levers

that work the switches. The switches and signals are so cleverly wired together that there is never any danger of one train's getting in another's way.

Towermen have telephones connected with other towers. These telephones are also connected with all the stations along the division. And all are connected with the office of the **train dispatcher** at the division point.

The train dispatcher is the man who orders the trains to move, or **dispatches** them. When a towerman or station operator telephones him that a train has safely passed a station or a signal tower, the dispatcher writes it down on a big paper called the **train sheet.** He knows where all the trains in his division are all the time.

A train dispatcher really gets busy when an **extra train** comes through. This may be a trainload of grain or fresh fruit that has to be moved quickly. Or it may be a trainload of soldiers, or boys and girls traveling to summer camp. The dispatcher has to **route** this train, or plan a way for it, through all the regular traffic. When he has done this, he telephones orders to the towermen and **station operators**—the men on duty in the stations. The towermen and operators copy these orders on thin paper called **flimsies.** A flimsy may read like this—"No. 42 east take siding at Tower KJ for Extra 146 east."

43

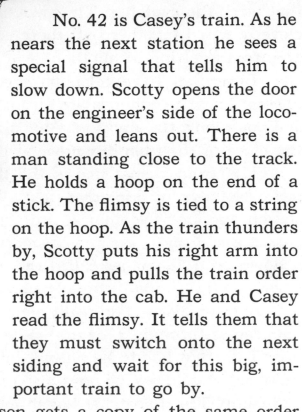

No. 42 is Casey's train. As he nears the next station he sees a special signal that tells him to slow down. Scotty opens the door on the engineer's side of the locomotive and leans out. There is a man standing close to the track. He holds a hoop on the end of a stick. The flimsy is tied to a string on the hoop. As the train thunders by, Scotty puts his right arm into the hoop and pulls the train order right into the cab. He and Casey read the flimsy. It tells them that they must switch onto the next siding and wait for this big, important train to go by.

Conductor Jackson gets a copy of the same order from a second hoop that the station man holds up when the caboose comes by.

Engineer Casey and Conductor Jackson will do exactly as the dispatcher orders. And they will not be surprised if a towerman sends them a new flimsy before they leave the siding. This may tell them to go ahead on a completely new schedule!

Some dispatchers now work through a wonderful new electric signaling and switching system. This is called **C.T.C.**—which is short for Centralized Traffic Control. The dispatcher sits in front of a panel that bristles with levers and push buttons. At the top of the panel is a lighted map of the tracks. Small lights on the map show where all the trains in the C.T.C. division are, even those on tracks miles away. The dispatcher watches the lights. By moving the levers on the control board he can throw the switches ahead of the trains so that the trains take the sidings and crossovers, pass and are passed by other trains without having to slow down for orders. As the switches move, the signals change, too.

The railroad yard

At the end of its run, Casey drives his train into the railroad terminal. Every train begins in one terminal and ends in another. The biggest yards are at terminals, junctions, and division points. These yards have special tracks and buildings where cars and engines are cleaned and repaired. Trains are broken up and cars are made into new trains. The diesel locomotives get fresh tankfuls of fuel oil, lubricating oil, sand, and water. Refrigerator cars get new supplies of ice, and tank cars get a good cleaning on the inside with steam. Often trucks drive into the yard to take loads from standing freight cars.

MAIN LINE

◄ "POCKET" TRACK FOR YARD ENGINES

THIS TRACK FOR YARD ENGINES TO GET BACK AND FORTH

YARD ENTRANCE

TRAIN BYPASSES YARD ON TH

All the different groups of tracks in a yard have names. These names tell what the tracks are for. Trains switch off the main line onto the **receiving tracks**. The locomotive uncouples and goes to the **engine tracks**. A switch engine takes the caboose to the **caboose storage tracks** while Conductor Jackson takes the car waybills

CABOOSE TRACKS

IN YARDS WITHOUT A HUMP SWITCH ENGINES PUSH CARS ALL THE WAY INTO THE CLASSIFICATION TRACKS

INSPECTION PITS, WHERE MEN SIT UNDER THE TRACKS AND INSPECT THE TRUCKS AND BRAKE GEAR

"BAD ORDER" CAR

YARD ENGINE SHOVES FREIGHT CARS OVER THE HUMP

TO ENGINE TERMINAL

THIS TRAIN WON'T BE BROKEN UP, BUT WILL BE INSPECTED AND SENT ON ITS WAY

MAIN LINE

to the **yardmaster,** or boss of the yard. Later, the cars are made up into new trains on the **classification tracks**, and then the new train leaves the yard on the **outbound** or **departure tracks.**

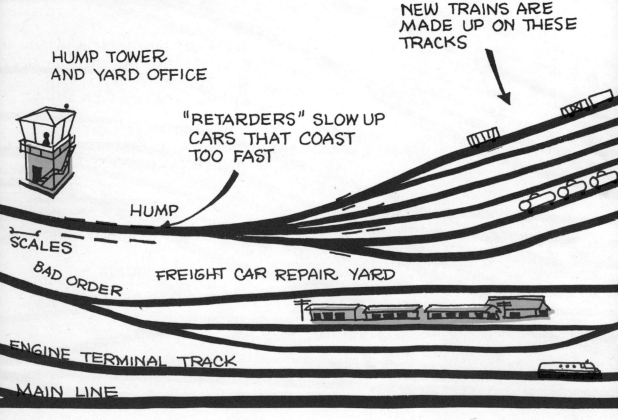

NEW TRAINS ARE
MADE UP ON THESE
TRACKS

HUMP TOWER
AND YARD OFFICE

"RETARDERS" SLOW UP
CARS THAT COAST
TOO FAST

HUMP

SCALES

BAD ORDER

FREIGHT CAR REPAIR YARD

ENGINE TERMINAL TRACK

MAIN LINE

48

While the cars are being sorted out and before they are made into new trains, Yardmaster Carr and his helpers make a **switching list.** This tells the number and weight of every car and where it is going. It also tells the number of the yard track where each car belongs.

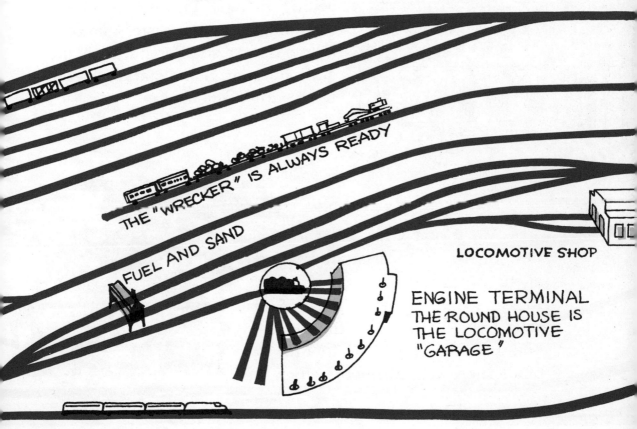

THE "WRECKER" IS ALWAYS READY

FUEL AND SAND

LOCOMOTIVE SHOP

ENGINE TERMINAL
THE ROUND HOUSE IS
THE LOCOMOTIVE
"GARAGE"

49

Who's who at the station

A city station may be an enormous terminal covering several city blocks. In the country it may be only a small building where one railroader does everything from sweeping the floor to selling tickets. The boss of a big station is called the **stationmaster.** The boss of a smaller station is the station agent. Some station agents today are women.

Mary and Greg are the station agent and assistant station agent of a medium-sized station. Mary works in the office. She sells tickets, gives out timetables, and answers questions. In Mary's office there is a telephone which is

50

connected with other telephones in stations all along the railroad. When a train on its way to Mary's station leaves another station, the agent telephones Mary to tell her it is on its way. Mary knows exactly when every train will arrive and when it will leave. Station agents used to send this information by telegraph. That is why agents are also called **telegraphers,** or operators.

Mary writes all the train information she receives on a bulletin board in the waiting room. Big stations also have a public address system over which the agents can announce when trains are due. This system is usually wired to lunch rooms, dining rooms, waiting rooms and all the station platforms. Greg can do the same work

Mary does, but he acts as baggage man, too. Jim is the **express agent.** If you want to send a package by Railway Express, Jim or one of his assistants will pick it up right at your home.

Mr. Smith works in the railroad's own freight office. He and his assistants make out the waybills for every freight car and freight shipment that leaves the station. The **freight house,** where cars are loaded and unloaded, is usually attached to the station. But sometimes it is a separate building with sidings. These sidings are alongside platforms that are built the same height as the car floors.

Railroaders you don't often see

There are many important railroaders that you are not likely to see very often. Railroad presidents, vice-presidents, supervisors, and hundreds of clerks and secretaries work in offices in the big stations and terminals. Then there are business agents who travel from place to place to get business for the railroads. And there are special clerks and secretaries whose job it is to keep records of what the railroad does from day to day, and where the railroad's cars are on other railroads. There are railroad lawyers, railroad doctors, and railroad advertising and publicity people. There are railroad detectives and policemen, too!

53

GRAND CENTRAL STATION on 42nd Street, New York City, has two underground train yards, one on top of the other. They have trackage enough for 200 outbound trains an hour. The enormous main concourse is one of the largest rooms in the world. The New York Central and the New Haven Railroads share this terminal.

KICKING HORSE RIVER

SPIRAL TUNNELS of the Canadian Pacific Railway loop the loop twice in the mountainsides of Kicking Horse River valley in British Columbia.

54

KNIGHT'S KEY BRIDGE, called "the eighth wonder of the world," spans seven miles of open water off the coast of Florida. Trains of the Florida East Coast's 128-mile Key West Extension steamed completely out of sight of land while crossing it. The tracks were damaged by a hurricane in 1935 and never replaced. U. S. Highway No. 1 now crosses the bridge.

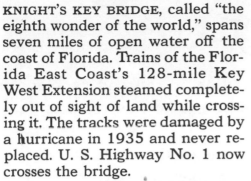

One of the WORLD'S HIGHEST RAILROAD BRIDGES soars 321 feet above the Pecos River in Texas. The quarter-mile bridge is on the Southern Pacific Railroad.

55

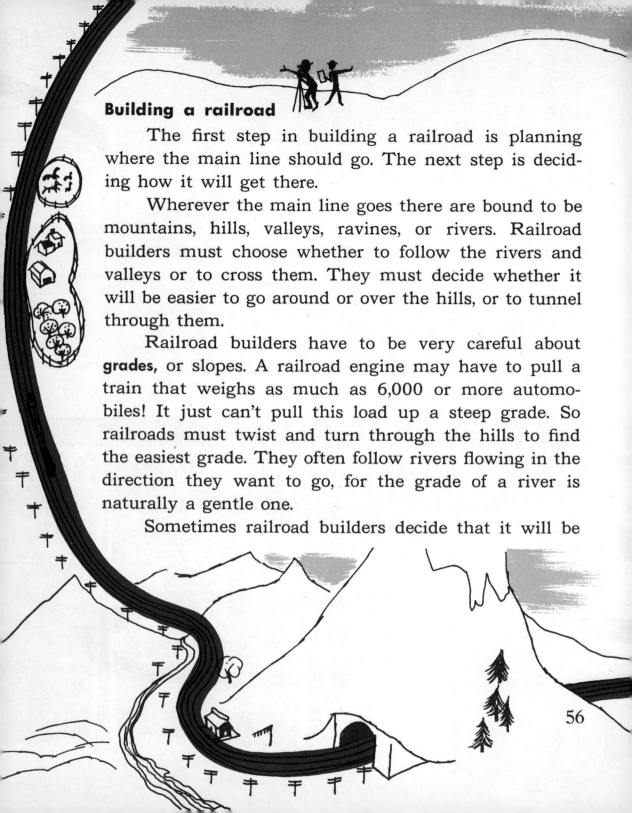

Building a railroad

The first step in building a railroad is planning where the main line should go. The next step is deciding how it will get there.

Wherever the main line goes there are bound to be mountains, hills, valleys, ravines, or rivers. Railroad builders must choose whether to follow the rivers and valleys or to cross them. They must decide whether it will be easier to go around or over the hills, or to tunnel through them.

Railroad builders have to be very careful about **grades,** or slopes. A railroad engine may have to pull a train that weighs as much as 6,000 or more automobiles! It just can't pull this load up a steep grade. So railroads must twist and turn through the hills to find the easiest grade. They often follow rivers flowing in the direction they want to go, for the grade of a river is naturally a gentle one.

Sometimes railroad builders decide that it will be

better to level the land along the way. They may cut away part of a hill at one place, and use the dirt from the **cut** to fill up a valley somewhere else. You will see cuts and **fills** all along many railroads.

Then there are always rivers that have to be crossed. And there are valleys too deep to fill with earth. That is why there are so many railroad bridges of different kinds and sizes.

Because trains are so heavy, railroad builders must lay the tracks on very solid ground. In the fills, they are careful to slope the sides of the packed earth evenly. This is so that it will not wash away. Then they put a layer of crushed stone—called **ballast**—under and around the ties to hold them in place. In the cuts, along hillsides, and even on level land, they make shallow **ditches** close to the ballast. Sometimes they also install **drain pipes** or make **culverts**—covered drains. These are put in so that water will flow away from the track quickly after a storm, leaving it firm and dry.

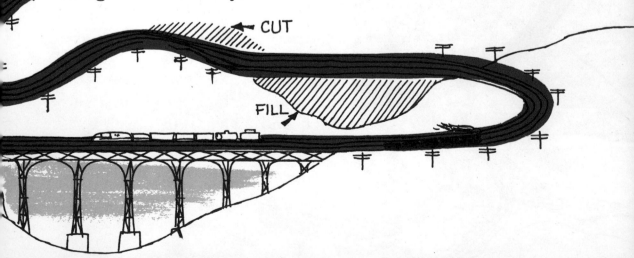

Taking care of the tracks

DETECTOR CAR

Twenty-four hours a day railroaders called **track inspectors** keep watch over the tracks to see that nothing goes wrong. **Detector cars**—which carry electronic instruments to find hidden flaws in rails—search out damaged or worn sections of track.

The minute the inspectors find something wrong they notify the repairmen. Then the **track gangs** swarm onto the tracks to mend them.

In the winter, out come the **snow plows.** If there is a light snow, simple, wedge-shaped plows shove the snow off the tracks. But sometimes the snow lies deep enough in the cuts to bury whole trains. Then the locomotives push giant **rotary plows** through the drifts. In front of the plows are great whirling blades that throw the snow high and away from the line.

SNOW PLOW

Flangers are metal scrapers hung underneath a plow or special car to clear the rails of lumps of snow and ice. In the yards, railroaders burn fires at the switch points to keep the switches thawed out and working smoothly.

Then there are men and machines to cut down weeds and clear the ditches along the tracks. Others spread new ballast, root out old ties and lay new rails. Signalmen, steelworkers, painters, electricians and carpenters all work at keeping the railroad and all the things along it in perfect working order.

ROTARY SNOW PLOW

WEED KILLER

BALLAST DISTRIBUTOR

Railroads in America

Railroads in America began as short lines running inland from coastal cities such as Boston, Philadelphia, Charleston and Baltimore. Lines also ran from river cities like Albany and New Orleans. In 1833 the longest railroad in the world ran from Charleston to Hamburg, South Carolina. This railroad was 136 miles long.

The tracks on these early railroads were made of strap-iron on wood. At first horses pulled the trains. One of the first railroads in America was the Granite Railway, a three-mile stretch of track laid down to help build Bunker Hill monument. Horses or mules pulled carloads of granite uphill in one direction, then rode back in the cars they had pulled up!

The first passenger cars were built like stage coaches. The freight cars were like small four-wheeled wagons or carts.

The Iron Horse

Then something happened that made a great difference in railroading. Back in 1769 an English inventor named James Watt had made an engine that ran by steam power. Now railroaders put a steam engine on a car with extra big wheels—and called it a locomotive. Now there was power to pull loads easier and faster than they had ever been pulled before.

In 1830 a steam locomotive raced a horse. It lost the race only because part of its machinery broke down just as it was beginning to win. But the race proved that steam power was more than enough to pull trains.

By 1840 steam locomotives were very familiar sights. Americans called them **iron horses.** No other machines ever seemed so much alive as these. The steam locomotives thundered over the land with their great driving wheels rolling, their side rods dancing, smoke and steam billowing overhead or streaming back along the following cars. From the drum-roll of a racing express to the panting choo-choo-choo of a loaded freight on a steep grade, Americans have lived to the sound of the iron horse for over a hundred years. During that time the electric locomotive was invented, and ran on some lines. But Americans never loved it as they did the steam locomotive.

61

STEAM LOCOMOTIVES

Steam locomotives have been in use on American railroads for more than a hundred years. A special tank car, the **tender**, coupled to each engine carries fuel and water. A coal or oil fire changes the water to steam in the tube-shaped **boiler** over the driving wheels. Then, fed into the cylinders, the hot, expanding steam pushes the **pistons** and **rods** to make the wheels turn.

TENDER   LOCOMOTIVE

SMOKESTACK

BELL

BOILER

CAB

PILOT, OR "COWCATCHER"

RODS
DRIVING
WHEELS   CYLINDER

62

The "Northern" is a
4-8-4

The "Hudson" is a 4-6-4

Trainmen classify loco-
motives by the arrange-
ment of their wheels
from front to back.

The "Berkshire" is a
2-8-4

A wood-burning steam
locomotive of the 1860's

A six-wheel switcher

63

The search for safety

Steam made the trains go, but once they were moving it was hard to make them stop. In the early days, when an engineer wanted to slow or stop his train, he **whistled for brakes.** He gave a short, sharp "toot" on the whistle. Immediately every trainman rushed to the roofs of the freight cars or the platforms of the passenger cars. There they pulled on the brakes by hand.

Stopping a train this way didn't always work. Some times heavy freight trains got away from the trainmen on steep hills. Then the whole train would pile up at the first sharp curve. It was not until George Westinghouse patented the **air brake** in 1869 that people could begin to feel really safe riding in trains.

An air brake works by compressed air which is controlled by a lever in the engine cab. When the engineer moves this lever, the brakes on the engine and every car in the train go on.

In 1893 Congress made a law that all trains must have these air brakes. It also made a law that trains must have the automatic couplers already invented by Eli Hamilton Janney. Before these couplers were used, trainmen had to stand between the cars and couple them by hand. Many trainmen were hurt and some were killed when something went wrong or it was too dark to see.

64

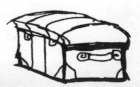

The first railroad to cross the continent

Although there were many railroads in America by 1850, there was none that went all the way across the country. A railroad from the Atlantic Ocean to as far west as the Great Lakes at Buffalo opened in 1851. Five years later, the railroaders built the first bridge over the Mississippi at Davenport, Iowa. In 1867 a line pushed across Iowa to Council Bluffs, opposite Omaha. There the railroad stopped.

In 1862, President Abraham Lincoln had signed an act that gave permission to build a railroad from the Missouri River to the Pacific Ocean. The act said that two companies should build this railroad. One was the new Union Pacific Railroad Company. The other was a railroad already running in California—the Central Pacific. The Union Pacific was to build track west out of Omaha while the Central Pacific built track east out of California.

With all the great mountains and rivers and prairies in the way, this was a giant task. The Central Pacific brought workers from China to build the grades that would conquer the mountains. These workers bored Summit Tunnel through a quarter mile of solid rock on the highest mountain. When winter came, snow buried the roadbed thirty feet deep. Four times avalanches pushed whole construction camps—men, buildings, and supplies—down the mountainsides. They lay buried there until spring.

The Union Pacific hired mostly Irish workers and veterans who had worked at track building in the Civil War. Often these workers had to throw down their tools and pick up guns to fight the warlike Sioux Indians.

For five years the railroad builders worked. By late 1867 the Central Pacific was in Nevada, and the Union Pacific was in the Rocky Mountains at Sherman, Wyoming. Then one of the strangest races in history began.

The government had offered rewards in land and bonds for each mile of track the railroads built. So each railroad wanted to build as many miles as possible. Each built just as fast as the men could work until the railroads ran past each other, side by side!

Back in Washington, the government decided that the two railroads should join tracks at Promontory, Utah. A great celebration was arranged for May 10, 1869. On that day, with great ceremony, railroaders hammered in the golden spike that joined the rails. Then, before the cheering crowd, locomotive Jupiter of the Central Pacific and locomotive Number 110 of the Union Pacific steamed proudly down the tracks toward each other. They touched pilots over the golden spike to mark the spanning of this whole great continent by the long steel rails.

Railroad Talk

Air Brakes—wind (or) the wind
Any Railroader—a rail
Box Car—sidedoor pullman
Caboose—cage, crummy, dog house, hack, hearse, hut, louse cage, monkey house, palace, parlor, shanty
Car Inspector or **Repair Man**—car toad
A Crossover—a diamond
Cupola Of Caboose—crow's nest
Damaged Car—cripple
Dispatcher—train detainer, de-layer, master mind
Engineer—eagle-eye, hogger, hog head, pig mauler, throttle art-ist
Fast Freight—hotshot, red ball, manifest
Fast Passenger Train—highliner, hotshot
Fireman—bakehead, fireboy, stoker, tallowpot, bell ringer
Freight Train—rattler
Freight Yard—the garden
Main Line—high iron, main iron, main stem
Overheated Bearing, where wheel axle rolls in a truck frame—hot box

Passenger Cars—the varnish
Passenger Coaches—cushions
Pullman Car—the varnish
A Railroad—pike
A Signal—the board
Semaphore Signal—a paddle
Signal To Proceed—highball
Speed Recorder—tattletale
Steam Locomotive—hog, pig, mill, calliope, smoker, battleship
Switch—gate
Throw A Switch—bend the iron
To Take Siding—go in the hole
Track Worker—gandy dancer, snipe
Train Conductor—big O, the brains, captain, king, skipper
Train Pulled By Two Locomotives—double-header
Train Order—flimsy
Waybill—willie
Way Freight—peddler
Wrecked or **Derailed**—in the ditch
Wrecking Crane—big hook
Yard Engine—goat
Yardmaster—ringmaster
Yard Office—beehive

Index